Different Kinds of Rock

Rocks can be formed by Earth's crust. Sometimes ro deposited in water. Some rock formations occur under pressure. Movements of the Earth's surface can create mountains of rock.

Magma, or molten rock, from the Earth's core is forced into layers of rock as it moves upward. The minerals from the magma form veins in the rock. The veins appear as different-colored layers. It is **characteristic** for these veins to contain ores such as gold and silver.

5

Volcanoes are one example of how igneous rock is formed. Hot lava, or melted rock, pours from a volcano. When it cools, it forms igneous rock.

Some rock is called sedimentary rock because it is formed by layers of sediments, which are materials deposited in lakes and oceans. Water can make rocks **corrode**, or fall apart. The corroded matter gets swept into the water, along with sand and minerals. Over long periods of time, these layers get pressed together and harden into sedimentary rock.

Another kind of rock is called metamorphic rock. The word *metamorphic* means "to change." A metamorphic rock forms when another rock—igneous, sedimentary, or even metamorphic—is changed due to heat or pressure. The heat might come from volcanic action, or the pressure might come from earthquakes that cause the Earth's crust to move with great force.

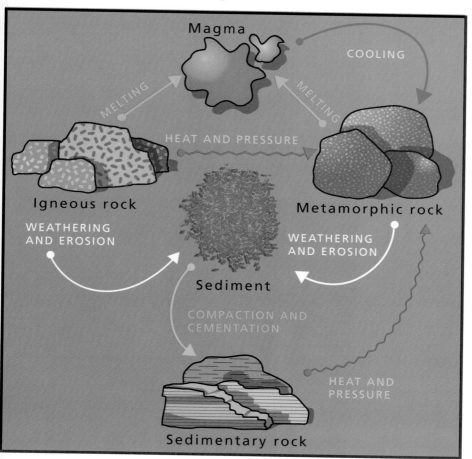

Rocks Give Us Minerals

As humans began to understand more about the many different minerals in the ground, they began to develop mining techniques for removing those minerals. Early civilizations are named for metals that were created from rocks or minerals removed from the ground.

The Bronze Age lasted for about 2,000 years. It ended at about 1,000 B.C. During this period, many objects were made of bronze, a metal alloy made from copper and tin. The Iron Age followed the Bronze Age. It marks the period when people learned to **extract** iron from rock. Miners built furnaces to melt the iron in the rock. They also worked with the iron by heating it and shaping it with hammers.

Scientists have found copper mines that are several thousand years old.

This ancient copper mine in Wales is about 3,500 years old. The mine has narrow tunnels in it where Bronze Age people dug for copper-bearing rock. They used stone hammers. It is believed that children did most of the mining. There are also larger chambers where adults would have been able to work.

Mining and the Romans

Mining was very important to the Romans. The wealth of their empire was built by trading minerals that included tin, copper, gold, and silver.

The Romans carried on mining in all parts of their empire. They used hammers, iron bars, and picks to break the rock that contained the minerals. The broken rock would be put into large baskets and carried out of the mine.

The Romans knew how to construct a shaft, or opening, to lead down to the silver or gold mine. Shafts brought enough air into the underground tunnels and chambers so that the workers would not choke or become too hot. Miners lit underground areas with oil lamps like the ones in their homes.

The Romans also made a system of pumps to control water that came from aquifers—underground layers of water-bearing rock. Without these pumps, the mines would have been **engulfed** by the water and flooded.

The Romans knew how to construct complicated underground mines. There they found gold and silver, two of the most valuable minerals.

Roman Pumps

The Roman pumps were operated by men who turned great wheels. They would grasp a handle or walk along steps built into the wheel. Each step caused the wheel to turn.

The purpose of the wheel was to scoop up water in buckets that were fastened to the wheel's rim. The water was then dumped into a container that could be emptied.

One kind of pump did not actually pick up water by using buckets. Instead, it moved water along a line of large wooden screws.

The water followed the channels in the screws as they were turned by a large wheel. The screw was placed inside a pipe that carried the water to the surface or to a tank where it was stored.

This kind of pump used a series of large wooden screws called Archimedes screws, named after the man who invented them.

Gold and Silver

The Romans learned to **exploit** valuable minerals, such as gold and silver, wherever they could find them. Often the minerals were scarce and hard to extract.

The Romans overcame this problem by building great bonfires inside a mine. As the gold or silver melted, it was much easier to collect. However, for people working in the mines, the heat and fumes were very dangerous and uncomfortable.

Flecks of gold can
be seen in this rock.

The basic layout of modern mines and the way minerals are extracted from the Earth are similar to the layout and techniques of ancient mines. The big difference today is the use of power-driven machinery to extract and transport mineral-rich ore.

Today we have deep, underground mines much like the Roman mines. Underground mines are generally for extracting precious metals—gold and silver—or nonmetallic minerals such as diamonds or coal.

New machines and techniques have made mining and smelting easier and more effective.

Slope Mine

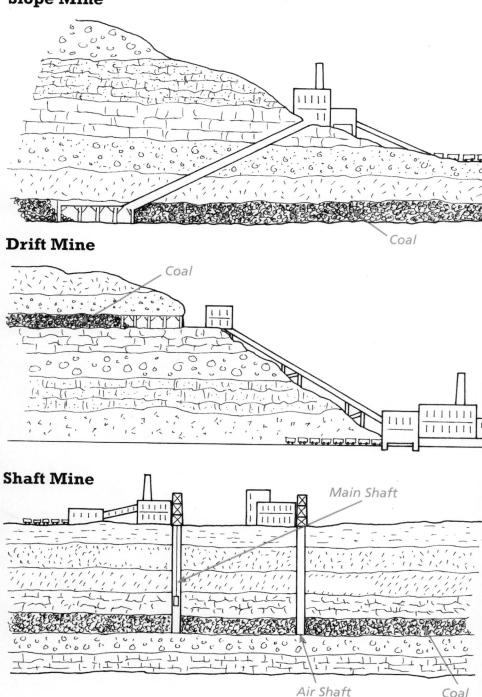

Coal

Drift Mine

Coal

Shaft Mine

Main Shaft

Air Shaft

Coal

Different Kinds of Mines

There are several different kinds of mines. Slope mines are built into the side of a hill above a mineral vein. A slope mine has a shallow tunnel that slopes down to the minerals.

A drift mine is built into a hillside. The mining there is done directly into the hill.

The most complicated and dangerous mine is the deep underground shaft mine. A shaft mine has a vertical tunnel and an elevator that carries workers down to the area where the minerals are found. Another shaft, called an airshaft, provides air to the workers. The airshaft also carries away the poisonous gases that are often found in mines.

A gold mine in Zimbabwe, Africa

17

Other Mines

When minerals are close to the Earth's surface, a surface mine is built. Such mines can be in water. Miners rinse sand or silt in a container. Because minerals such as gold, silver, and tin are heavier than sand or silt, they end up on the bottom of the container.

Miners of the Gold Rush in the mid-1800s extracted gold from sand by panning. The sand was washed until the gold was left at the bottom of the pan.

Another kind of surface mine is an open-pit mine. In the state of Utah, there is an enormous open-pit copper mine.

The process of removing the copper-rich ore is started by drilling holes into rock and blasting the rock with special powder. Then huge mechanical shovels pick up the ore. It is loaded into trucks and taken to another part of the mine. First it is crushed and exposed to chemicals that remove the copper. Then the copper is melted. The melted copper travels along a pipe for about 15 miles, where it is made into pure copper. Gold and silver are also extracted from the ore and made into bars.

This open-pit mine in Utah is two-and-a-half-miles wide and a half-mile deep.

Rare and Valuable

Coal is a fairly common mineral. Other minerals are rare. They attract attention. Sometimes people **hoard** rare minerals or trade them illegally.

A diamond, although dark and gray when it is taken from the earth, becomes a sparkling gem in the hands of an expert cutter. Diamonds are very hard. Besides being prized for their beauty, they have valuable industrial uses. They can cut and help grind other minerals.

Throughout history, diamonds have been taken as a prize of war or given to kings or queens as a sign of respect.

Diamonds are mined in southern
Africa in very deep mines.

Diamonds are composed of pure carbon and found in only a few places worldwide. The ore containing the diamond is blasted from the mine wall. Heavy equipment is used to crush and haul the ore to a nearby plant where it is processed. The diamonds are extracted from the ore and graded for quality.

Other Precious Minerals

The mineral corundum is also a source of beautiful jewels. Corundum is a grainy-looking, reddish mineral that has hidden within it the beautiful and colorful family of gems called sapphires. Some are deep blue. The red gems are called rubies. There are also yellow and pink sapphires.

Corundum is only slightly less hard than diamonds. Corundum that contains gem sapphires is found among gravel, especially in Asia. It is mined in surface mines.

Rocks and minerals come in many shapes, sizes, and colors.

Summary

We use rock for many purposes. The minerals that make up rock are used in everyday industries as well as in beautiful jewelry.

People are fascinated by minerals, whether they are diamonds, rubies, or copper. There is a sense of mystery around rocks and minerals. Maybe we are attracted to the idea that they are found deep within the Earth. Maybe we appreciate the hard work that it takes to mine minerals. Or maybe we feel a connection that is historical—a connection to generations of people who mined our planet's ground long before we came along.

Glossary

characteristic *adj.* special; distinctive.

corrode *v.* to wear or eat away gradually.

engulfed *v.* overwhelmed or submerged.

exploit *v.* to make use of.

extract *v.* to draw out.

hoard *v.* to save and store away.